Whispers of Krip Love
Shouts of Krip Revolution

Poetry by

Lateef H. McLeod

Other Works by Lateef H. McLeod
A Declaration of a Body of Love

Cover Art and Graphic Design by Monique Harris
See more of her work on her website:
http://www.moniqueharriscreations.website/.

ISBN: 978-1-7337025-6-0

Printed in the United States of America

Poetic Matrix Press
www.poeticmatrix.com

Whispers of Krip Love
Shouts Of Krip Revolution

For my Mom

Your constant love and encouragement
gave me the strength and determination
to write and publish this book.

Why you fear me?
Why you freak out whenever I am around?
What is it about the sight of me that makes you cringe?
Is it because when you look at me you see
a reminder of your own fragility?
The fact that one day your body will go weak
and die decomposing into dust.

— Lateef H. McLeod,
"Why are you scared of me?"

Contents

Whispers of Krip Love
Shouts Of Krip Revolution

Part One: The Shout of Krip Rebellion

Part Two: Whether to Take a Knee or Raise a Fist

Part Three: Love Notes From A Lonely Krip

Part Four: The Krip Undress

About the Author

Whispers of Krip Love
Shouts Of Krip Revolution

PART ONE:

THE SHOUT OF KRIP REBELLION

I Am Too Pretty for Some "Ugly Laws"

I am not supposed to be here
in this body,
here
speaking to you.
My mere presence
of erratic moving limbs
and drooling smile
used to be scrubbed
off the public pavement.

Ugly laws used to be
on many U.S. cities' law books,
beginning in Chicago in 1867,
stating that "any person who is
diseased, maimed, mutilated,
or in any way deformed
so as to be an unsightly or disgusting object,
or an improper person to be allowed
in or on the streets, highways, thoroughfares,
or public places in this city,
shall not therein or thereon
expose himself to public view,
under the penalty of $1 for each offense." [1]
Any person who looked like me
was deemed disgusting
and was locked away
from the eyes of the upstanding citizens.

I am too pretty for some Ugly Laws,
Too smooth to be shut in.
Too smart and eclectic
for any box you put me in.
My swagger is too bold
to be swept up in these public streets.

You can stare at me all you want.
No cop will bust in my head
and carry me away to an institution.
No doctor will diagnose me
a helpless invalid with an incurable disease.
No angry mob with clubs and torches
will try to run me out of town.
Whatever you do,
my roots are rigid
like a hundred-year-old tree.
I will stay right here
to glare at your ugly face too.

---

[1] Quote from *The Ugly Laws* by Susan M. Schweik

Ten AAC Commandments –
Notorious B.I.G. Style

"It is the Ten AAC[2] Commandments. Whaaaat...?"

I have been in the AAC game for years
until I studied every granule.
This form of communication has rules
so I wrote me a manual.
A step-by-step booklet for you to get
your speech on track
so you won't get left back.
Rule number One:
If you are on the run,
always make sure your device is charged
or else you will have no fun.
Especially
if you meet
that special someone on the street
that you want to take out to eat.
Number Two:
Always have essential, instant phrases preprogrammed,
so you will have a quick saying
for someone you don't mind dating.
If you fumble with your typing
the person you like will end up walking.
You will end up looking dumb
talking to air like a bum.

---

[2]Augmentative Alternative Communication

Number Three:

Never let anyone talk for you unless it is necessary.

Even if your mom wants to speak for you,

like you don't have a clue.

And before you know it you have things done to you,

that will leave you feeling blue.

Number Four:

Now I know heard this before.

never roll around in your chair without your device secure on there.

Number Five:

Always charge your device at night

or else your device will be shut down like a vice.

Number Six:

Never let your friends play with your device.

Remember the device represent your voice and is not a toy alright?

Number Seven:

This rule is so underrated.

keep your meals and your device completely separated.

If any food or drink fall into the inner workings of your device while it's unprotected,

it will short circuit the whole thing leaving you stranded.

Number Eight:

Always clear previous conversations

to avoid saying things again that was not your intention.

Number Nine:

This should have been Number One to me.

Make sure you have a good evaluation from your SLP[3].

She is the one who will recommend the right device for you.

So treat her right because

she is an essential member of your crew.

Number Ten:

Pick your role models who use AAC carefully.

Knowing that if you watch them daily

you will eventually see

you will be where they be.

Then other kids will look up to you,

so you'd better be on your p's and q's.

Follow these rules and you will master your AAC

and will be able to talk to anybody.

Look around and you will see

that no one can break it down better than me.

---

[3] Speech Language Pathologists

Invisible Man, Revisited

I am the transparent mirage in your mind's eye.
The image you want to hold,
but with time
will simply forget.

You think you see me.
Can visualize and grasp
who I am.
In a wheelchair, yes.
Use an AAC device to speak, yes.
Has cerebral palsy, yes.
Was educated at UC Berkeley and Mills, yes.
Still you will not see me.

Because that is just the mask
that the real me hides behind
to give you that false security,
that my life is OK.
Must be OK!
I am a productive, working, taxpayer.
It must be OK.

But if I take off the mask
to reveal my true facial features.
Let you see how my family and friends
take me for granted
and barely stay in contact with me.

I am always the odd man out.
The one left out of informal gatherings
of friends chatting about old times
over good food.
Or even formal gatherings,
"You are going to this party right?
Everyone is going."
I am like, "What party?"
I must have missed that on my Facebook scroll."

When close friends marry,
I am invited.
Of course, there is no room in the bridal party.
I'm always one place removed from
the close circle of intimate community,
always
an orphan hugging myself in the wind.

When will I be accepted into relationships
where I am called when you need someone
to talk,
laugh,
or cry to?
What trial must I triumph
so that the scales fall from your eyes?
Because if I am invisible for too long,
I might totally disappear for good.

Why the Fuck I Am Angry

If you are wondering
why my anger spews up
like a boiling black kettle,
you can go no further then
the construction of this society,
my own community was made to exclude me.

I was an after thought,
after someone somewhere
devised a mechanic way to speak.
I was reluctantly gained admittance
into the circle of humanity

I was told if I just got a good education
and obtained a good occupation
that I will be accepted and respected
as a professional and personal man in my community.
As I grew up,
the shit of the American Dream smeared all over me
and made me reek.
I was still left off in the cold.

Of course I got angry,
Like an inferno swelling up in my gut
waiting to burst out and be birthed on the world.
My desire to unleash my fury ate at my soul.
My mother's fright and tears

made me swallow my fury back in,
where it consumes me slowly.

I am a man seen as a boy,
because my self-righteous rage
is only seen as
an overgrown temper tantrum.

It Wasn't My Fault

I was just thirsty.
It wasn't my fault
that I disturbed you
from your intimate time
with your phone.

I didn't want to show off
in front of my girlfriend,
who just came out of the bathroom
and most likely did not see my gestures anyway.

I don't know how you felt less than human
when I gestured to you, my attendant,
that we must leave the movie theater.
Yes, I was in a hurry,
because, like I said, I was thirsty.

No, I don' know why you said you wanted to quit.
Like I said before, I only gestured to you.
I didn't yell,
scream,
curse,
or call you out by your name.
So, I don't know why you are in a huff
when I only want a drink.

Yes, I meant to call my mom,
because you acted illogical and immature

and I thought she could talk sense to you.
No, it wasn't appreciated that you called
someone to work the rest of the shift;
our argument was not that serious.

No, what you said to my sister and mom
about my girlfriend instigating the whole thing
was not true.
You know it's a lie,
I know it's a lie.
All that did was to get them both angry at me.
And then, to top it off,
after that, you left like a coward.

So, to turn a cool night with my girlfriend
to a night where my mom and sister
scolded me like a spoiled little kid
for offending you,
who really did act
like a spoiled little kid?
I always will remember
how you acted a fool
when I had cotton-mouth tongue
and only wanted a drink of water.

Why Do I Work?

Why do I work
in this non-essential job,
writing blogs for this website
that no one reads?

Why do I sit here at this computer,
day after day,
writing articles that I care minimally about,
published on a blog almost no one reads?

Why do I fill out a timesheet –
my hours of work –
for a late-to-come check
of a few hundred dollars?

I should use my talents
to script succinct poetry verses
for the sole purpose to spit them
at slams and open mics
for my adoring fans to hear!

I should be on the stage on Def Poetry Jam,
or at least Verses and Flow,
spitting out the slew of lyrics
to make me the household name
of the poet who came to master fame
and expose my intellect's wide range.

I should lock myself in a room
for at least five hours a day,
in mad scientist fashion,
unplugging phone and internet,
and delve deep into the art
of creating Frankenstein literature and poetry
until I bust out of my room with sweat on my brow
yelling "it's alive!"

I want my words desperately to be alive,
to penetrate waxed slicked ears with permission,
to linger with pleasure in the mind,
so a person can taste my thoughts on the tip of their tongue.

I want my words to dance in people's heads
until they burst out of people's mouths,
and salsa or linden hop into other people's poetry,
until it unleashes in a well spring of word and song
that not even the Hoover Dam can contain!

This job's joy surpasses any pay.
Just to see the twinkle in people's eye
is superior to the satisfaction of productivity of any job.

So I Am Still a Baby?

So even with my mustache and my deep voice
and muscular physique of bulging biceps, protruding
pectorals, and asphalt abs,
that prove without a doubt that I am a man.
Even with all my degrees,
my bachelor's in English
my master's in Creative Writing
my upcoming doctorate in Anthropology
that proves without a doubt that
I intellectually engage with anyone.
Even though I showed you my heart,
show you how much I cared and loved you
with all your smudges on your self-portrait.
You refuse to hoist
me up with you so I can seek
the same level as you...
so I can be free too.
Free so I can embrace you
my love
as your equal.

I Am All Right

Don't look at me
with that condescending smile –
that smile you give babies
that you think are adorable and naive.
My eyes were seared with the experience of life
and the must of maturity to ever be naive.
And only a young lady with a slim figure and a dimpled
smile
is allowed to caress my face.
For the rest of you,
I am not an adorable, cuddly teddybear
who you can pinch my cheeks until I coo.

I am not a ward of the state,
a helpless infantile.
Look at me and know that this man
works and pays bills
like you do.
Have a circle of friends and a social life
like you do.
Go on dates with those that I am attracted to
like you do.
My life is too profound and extraordinary for your pity.

Don't use me for some profile for some charity.
I am no Jerry Lewis kid.
Your money will not improve my life.

I don't need a doctor to come up with a cure
or a holy roller preacher to pray for my healing.
I am all right.

You can come and talk to me.
Come and have a conversation with me
about politics,
about sports,
about religion,
and we can delve into
the many facets
of each of those topics.
Let me talk about
the failure of our
two-political party system,
or how my Niners
will be going to the Super Bowl next year,
or why Jesus Christ
is my Lord and Savior.

Because I will then force you
to see me as the man
that I clearly am.

And You Can't See Me Now, Because...?

Why are you afraid of me?
Is it because I drool?
Because I talk with an AAC device,
am in a wheelchair?
Let's just say that you are afraid of my erratic
long flowing limbs
that my cerebral palsy gives a life of their own.

Is it because I am the symbol of
no self-control that scares you?
That my body rebels
against my brain's supposed iron grip over it,
and dares to run free with no master.
In this culture where a person is responsible
for controlling his circumstances,
especially his body,
his best corporal representation of this world.
My body defies all logic and moves to his own beat.

Is it because I fail your notion of what a man is?
That I don't stand and command
attention when I enter the room.
That I can't throw a ball or shoot a ball.
I sure can kick the ball with my chair,
but that is a different story.
But I am not a man's man.
Not a hard-to-get-knocked-down man.
Not a stare-you-down-if-you-disrespect-me man.

Is it because I am not a woman's ideal of a lover.
Not the chisel-chested Adonis specimen
that can pick you up with one arm?
Not the one who she can bend this way and that
in every Kama Sutra position imaginable.

Is it because when you see me,
you see your own mortality?
Too hard to see me because
you see yourself in my position when old,
in a wheelchair, drooling,
unable to go to the bathroom by yourself?
Is this why you try to avoid me,
because to recognize me would mean to see
the fragility of your body
staring back at you?
If my whole existence is somehow all about you.

Well let's get some things straight.
I don't exist to be your pity case.
Not here to be your inspiration,
your punching bag,
or your saint.

My life does not hold in the capacity of your conception.
It will burst out of any narrative you construct,
and I will recreate myself new again,
with more variety and depth.

I am the man who is in complete control of his body,
whose muscular physique,
is every straight woman's desire.
It is just a matter of perspective.

Why Are You Scared of Me?

As a child I knew I was
good,
adorable,
and safe.
Because that was what my parents told me,
that was what my grandma told me,
that was what my physical therapist told me,
that was what my teachers told me.
So I believed it.
I rolled around in my power wheelchair
with my head held high
and knew I was God's child, blessed with promised.

But the vision that I had of myself
was not always reflected back in the eyes of others.
From an early age people used to stare at me
and bore their eyes in the back of my skull,
like I was some freak,
some monster whose face is too grotesque to look at.

I grew up with kids who gawked at
my gangly limbs squirming in my chair
with an unease that never went away.
The kids' taunts taught lessons
of how I was out of place in their space.
Malicious words sprung off their tongues
and crashed into my eardrums,
along with their hate and indifference.

Why you fear me?
Why you freak out whenever I am around?
What is it about the sight of me that makes you cringe?
Is it because when you look at me you see
a reminder of your own fragility?
The fact that one day your body will go weak
and die decomposing into dust.

Or do you fear me for my skin?
The smooth maroon encasing of my body,
illicit fears that I might kick you,
hit you,
roll over you in my wheelchair.
Am I that nappy-headed criminal
that makes you clutch your purse
as you walk past me?
Do you secretly wish that a police officer
will come and bust in my head and take me to jail,
or better yet, put a bullet in my heart
to stop the enraged monster you see me as?

Or do you see me as a freak?
A monster whose body
medicine cannot fix.
Whose body cannot be loved,
cannot be sexually desired.
Cannot provide a woman
with her physical,
emotional,
spiritual,

and sexual needs.
Why does a woman emasculate me
with her gaze?

Do you see my body as only acceptable if rehabilitated?
If I am worked on in a surgical or therapeutic way
to fix me,
then you will embrace me with open arms,
because then I will be just like you?
That may look like a happy ending to you,
but you will never know why you are really scared of me.

Part Two
Whether to Take a Knee
or Raise a Fist

So Much

I hear their painful cries jut up from cracks on the street.
The block is a scorching frying pan,
frying my brothers on the pavement.
Our bodies are etched on the concrete,
blood drenched as permanent ink.
Chalk should not outline our deathbed
or a body bag be our first casket.

Bullets lurch out of guns,
slice the air, and
pierce the thin borders of our black skin.
Eat away at our muscle and bones,
borough through sinews and blood vessels,
until it reaches and stops our hearts.

It is not just the gang member on the corner
whose aim we have to dodge,
but also police on the beat
whose itchy trigger fingers
leave us with our brain matter
splattered on the concrete.

Now we have to watch out for
the neighborhood watchmen.
The wanna-be-cops who think
we are foreign to our own neighborhood.
Trayvon had a hoodie on to protect him from the rain,

but it didn't protect him
from the bullet from Zimmerman's gun.
Old George just couldn't help
being a deadly Don Quixote,
and shoot at every black boy,
claiming he was a harden criminal.

My coco skin is not a target for your gun.
It is the sacred encasing of God's masterpiece
that gives warmth and joy to every loved one it touches.
No bullet will destroy what God has made immortal.
We will all rise again one day to walk under the sun.

Who Will Protect the Young Black Boys in the Suburbs?

Who will protect us from you?
You who fear us,
because of our hoodies,
our loud hip hop,
our darker hue.
Our brash bravado
that does not bow to your whim,
your whip,
your baton.
Now our defiance is too much
that you cut us down with guns.

And we thought we were safe
if we move our sons into a nice neighborhood.
If we gave them a good education
and got them into a good school.
We as young men would be accepted,
not be a threat to you.

But even if we get an elite Stanford education,
and some swagger in on step
you are quick to call us a thug
if our tongues become too haughty for your liking.
Must be always even tempered and well mannered
less you deem us obnoxious.
Call us a gorilla

just because we turned up
in front of a prissy blonde white woman.
Are you for real?

You who have been killing us
ever since we got to this place.
Overworked to death
in those sugar and cotton plantations,
oil drenched whips
left blood strained streaks
down our backs.
We would cry with outstretched hands
as our sons and daughters were ripped from our grasp
and sold down the river.

You who devised an apartheid system after slavery
just to avoid being near us.
Where you made our men underpaid field hands,
our women domestic maids,
and made our boys into alligator bait.
For real, you made them alligator bait.

It was like you became addicted to killing us.
We became the bloodied strange fruit
swinging from southern trees.
You used to gather around
and watch the life
being strangled from us
right above you.

And no age was safe from your wrath.
Emmitt Till, 14 years old.
Beaten and pummeled beyond recognition
all because he whistled at a white woman.
Oscar Grant, 22 years old.
Handcuffed and pinned down
between Messerly's knee
and the Fruitvale Bart platform.
Murdered with a bullet shot in the back.
Trayvon Martin, just turned 17 years old.
Walking to his father's house
with a bag of Skittles,
minding his own business.
When George Zimmerman
stocked him,
accosted him,
threw him to the ground,
and shot him dead.

He said it was Trayvon's hoodie
that made Zimmerman think he was a criminal.
Alan Blueford, 18 years old.
Was chased by the police
and was shot down in cold blood
on these cold Oakland streets.
All because Alan ran
the cop gave the excuse
that he was up to no good.
Then there was Jordan Davis, 17 years old.

Who Michael Dunn murdered
just because Davis played loud hip-hop
in the car with his friends,
Dunn deemed them all thugs
and thought to kill them all
before they killed him.
Even though he was in no danger
from unarmed teenagers
from the suburbs.

Not one of the murders
of Emmitt, Oscar, Trayvon, Alan, or Jordan
were convicted of first-degree murder
in the first trials right after the crime,
and only the murder of Jordan Davis
eventually got the sentence
of life in prison.

It begs the question,
why are you scared of us
when you kill us
without much repercussion.
When you think about it,
the real monster to be feared
was always you.

We Are Not Sorry

The definition of being repentant is as follows:
expressing or feeling sincere regret and remorse.
In the bible to repent means
to acknowledge we have sinned,
are repulsed by our sin,
and actively turn away from our sin
to more righteous action.
In simplistic terms to repent means to change our ways.

What will it look like if we as a country
are truly sorry and repented from our sins?
What will it look like if turned away from all
the white supremacy, patriarchy,
ableism, and heteronormativity?
What will it look like if we really were sorry?

If we were sorry,
the Holocaust museum
will exhibit the Trail of Tears
as the one of the greatest blemishes
that America cannot wipe away from its memory.

If we were sorry,
Pine Ridge would not be
a poverty stricken reservation
but a protected and flourishing neighborhood.

If we were sorry,
the name
of the professional football team in D.C.
would not be a racial slur.

If we were sorry,
children from Pine Ridge
won't cut themselves,
maim themselves,
kill themselves
because people around them
hate their history,
hate their culture,
hate them.

If we were sorry, my young black brothers and sisters
would not have to cross themselves and pray
every time a police patrol car roll by
or walk the other way.

If we were sorry, the president will not play footsies
with Alt-Right white national terrorists.
We would not watch him support policies
that cut the skin for everybody
that is not white, christian, straight, able-bodied,
and is preferably well off.
If he is supposed to be representative
of our country's values,
then we know who is important to this country
and who is not.

You have to admit
that this country looks
like we are not sorry.

Father Capitalism and Mother Democracy

My American brothers and sisters,
I gathered you here today
to discuss an issue of vital importance.
You know the parental threat that I speak of.
How this father of ours has been exploiting us
from the time we were born until now.
Has he not tried to monetize
every single thing in our lives,
until we end up wondering what the cost of love is?

His toxic financial philosophy was our infant formula.
We lapped up being cost-effective
and having a bottom line
with our porridge as toddlers.
Our father Capitalism towers over us and makes sure we
wear out our muscles and bone in dutiful work
for dollars and cents, until we are used up
in body, spirit, and mind.

We are broken like our mother is broken,
our poor Mother Democracy.
Broken to our Father's will.
With the slap of Citizens United leaving
a scar on her face.
We weep as we couldn't protect her
as Glass-Steagall and Ergonomics
took the shackles off our Father and his furious rage.

And look how much our Mother nurtured us.
She has instilled in us sacred values
That our words are precious and vital to us
and that we need to listen to each others words
with open and understanding ears.
She made us believe
that if we all worked together
our country will be great.

It was her tender touch and encouragement
we were able to shake off
some of the vile evils of our Father.
From the bloody oiled-whipped backs
the victims of chattel slavery
to the pit of hell that was the factory a hundred years ago.
We as women, people of color, homosexuals,
transgender people, and people with disabilities
were able to punch holes and walk threw barriers
that our Father Capitalism put in front of us.

But, my brothers and sisters,
over the years we have seen as our Father grows stronger,
our precious Mother has grown weak
and her body atrophies under his vice grip.
It is time to face facts and search deep in ourselves.
Father Capitalism will kill our Mother Democracy
if given a chance.
So our choice is clear in light of this fact.
Our patricide will free our Mother to live on and thrive.

Self-Hatred

Why do you throw stones in your own reflection?
Trying to straighten out naps,
Squeeze noses down to size,
Use cake soap to lighten skin complexion
between Vybz Kartel and the late MJ.
While those with pale skins lay on the beach for a tan.

You, who memorize the lies
coming from bobbing heads
from CNN or Fox,
that you are a violent criminal,
welfare cheat,
deadbeat dad,
unfit mother.
Their images become ingrained in your psyche;
you make their stereotypes of you come true.

Every time you see a labeled criminal on television,
you cringe and hope
you don't have the same complexion.
You wear their shame as goosebumps on your arms,
as if their actions say something about your character.

You think if only they act more respectable
and spoke with good grammar,
then they could make something
of themselves as you have.
You, who went to the good schools

and obtained the good education.
You, who have a good job and a good home.
You, who think you obtained a piece of the American
Dream.
They just need to work harder
and they can be just like you.

Well, sorry to burst your bubble,
but they probably do not want to be you anyway.
Cuz you have not lifted a finger to help them.
You hardly spend money in their businesses
so we can have money in our local economy.
So eager you are to be Eurocentric,
you forget the Afrocentric.

Our history chock-full
with pharaohs building the pyramids of Kemit,
the stories from
the 15th century Catholic kingdom of the Kongo,
or the glory of the Akan and Oyo empires' kings.

Why do you want to identify
with a culture who
beats you,
rapes you,
sells you as commodities,
steals your names, language, and history,
and then ravages and pillages the very place
where you are from?

Think it may be time
to wipe the lightening makeup from your face,
let the kink come back in your hair,
and spend more time in the community
among people that will be willing to support you.
Love the coco skin you are in,
because it is the only one you got.

So, Why We Pledge Allegiance?

Why do we pledge allegiance to the state
that killed the peaceful King?
Because there is no doubt that the state killed him.
For he preached peace in a time of war they killed him.
For he advocated for justice and equality for the poor
in a time when society
admired and honored the rich,
they killed him.
For he loved his people
and fought for their total liberation,
they killed him.
Since this country killed our hero,
why do we pledge allegiance to it?

Pushing for Garvey

My brethren denied posthumous pardon
when first black president
passed him over
for politics.
Garvey was always for his people,
wanted to see all people of Africa rise like a phoenix,
whereas the president is a pushover in his positions,
flips his official posture like The Clapper
switches on and off the light...
as we the peasantry wait for a populace leader
that will save us from the coming plutocracy.

The History of Oppression

This how you make abuse and denigration normal.
First you attack the body.
Subjugate it,
Force it to do your will.
Once the body
is fully succumbed,
you work on the mind.
You have to make it see
you are the master.
Even thinking it ever could be
your equal is heresy.

You can't beat it too much,
you have to bring it close to you.
Caress its body,
kiss its body,
let it take down its guard
so when you violate and assault
its body again,
it will think it wanted it.
That it causes the abuse you drill into it.

You have to make it see itself as you see it.
An ugly, wretched thing totally void of anything to love.
You beat or fuck any sense of dignity
it once had until every thought it has of itself
comes from you.

You put a dog leash around its neck lined with diamonds
and it will smile because of the diamonds.
Then you will know it's yours.
But know this:
it has you too.

The Children

The news lies to you.
Telling you that it cares for children,
makes you care for certain children.
The babies that sweat and suffocate
in locked, parked cars we mourn.
However, if the babies are exploded,
pieces of their bodies,
splayed all over the Gaza street
by an Israeli missile,
then they are just collateral damage.
In the way of Israeli destruction
of Hamas rocket missiles.

The news tells you
that the death of these children are necessary.
Necessary to protect the Israeli children.
The news tells you
that the bombs falling from Israeli jets,
that blow to pieces mothers
nursing their babes on their breast,
are to keep Israeli mothers safe
in their gated commnities.

They tell you that every man
shot, beaten, and killed on the Gazan asphalt
is one less terrorist
that rain rockets on the innocent Israeli citizens.

You quickly turn the channel,
shaking your head, and wonder out loud
"If Israeli and Palestinians can ever get along?"
Totally oblivious to the fact that
you just witnessed apartheid and genocide in HD.

On the other channel you see children in school buses.
Children in school buses
with prison bars.
Children in school buses
with prison bars going to a detention center.
Children in school buses
with prison bars going to a detention center
while virulent Tea Partiers
yell racist slurs at them.
Children fleeing violence in their home country
due to American imperialist policies.
Yet still, do-nothing redneck Americans harass
these vulnerable young humans
as they are kicked out of the country.

The news tells you that these children are illegal.
The news tells you that these children have diseases.
The news tells you that these children do not belong here.
But if vulnerable children cannot capture a sanctuary
in this country,
then the question is, who can?

If after watching this you are at a loss of action
and think you can't do anything to make a difference
in these children's life.
That is where you are wrong,
because you can still save your empathy
by turning the lies of the TV news off
and get out in the street in a protest for love.

Make Me Understand

So, let me get this straight.
You don't know what they are out there for.
They who dare to occupy parks,
occupy plazas,
occupy sidewalks,
occupy streets,
of your neighborhood.
Right by your city hall,
right by your bank,
and you don't know what it is all for.
You don't see the point.
You say if they all just get up
and work,
it will all be alright.

Well, maybe you can make me understand.
Make me understand how they can look for work
when no jobs are to be found.
Make me understand how they can go home
when the banks foreclosed their homes.
Make me understand
how they will send their children to college
without going in debt for the rest of their lives.
Make me understand
how they can even afford a doctor when sick
without affordable healthcare.

Because I don't think we get it.
We just don't get how the rich
pay less percentage in taxes.
We don't get that
no one was put in prison for the bank crisis of '08.
We don't get why AIG got a big bail out and not us.

Make us understand
how police can
tear-gas a woman
running away from them.

Make us understand how
parks meant for the public are private property,
vacant houses from foreclosure are private property,
vacant lots not used by anyone are still private property

How is it that cities order their police
to beat us,
pepper spray us,
arrest us,
for just taking up space,
for being who we are.

They can do all they want,
We are not going anywhere.

Threat To Homeland Security

Don't get it twisted.
I'm a terrorist.
I am someone to be feared,
to be avoided.
Flee from me
when you see me
in the dark alleyways
at midnight.
Yes, please run from this crippled terrorist
who puts thoughts in your head
too awful to pronounce,
like, "What if I got around in a wheelchair like he does?"
or "What if I relied on an iPad to speak?"
or "Heaven forbid if I drooled a little in public!"

How dare I terrorize you
tonight in this club?
You see me gig in the club,
but this sight makes you uneasy
because I could get hurt
from the massing bodies around me,
because really,
isn't there a place for me
in some nursing home
where I will be supervised 24/7,
being fed industrial lime green jello
until I die?

Isn't this what all terrorists deserve,
to be locked away from public view
where we cannot harm or interact with
the innocent populace?
So what if a prisoner from Guantanamo Bay
gets water boarded?
So what if a person in a nursing home
gets to shower once a month?
It is what we deserve.

We should be locked away forever,
without charge or trial,
we with broken and proud bodies
that hold our heads high
so you can be safe
in the dark alleyways
at midnight.
Lock us up!
The other boogiemen —
the black criminal,
the illegal immigrant,
the Muslim extremist —
fill your jails and institutions
with our brown and black bodies
where they force feed us that industrial jello
until we puke up that green sloppy mess

Even in our peaceful protest
you see danger,

because if we prop up a tent in a park
in defiance
of our
stolen homes,
stolen jobs,
stolen wages,
you send in the cops
to beat our heads with billy clubs,
spray our eyes with mace,
strangle our wrists with cuffs,
because behind bars,
you can't hear our cries.

You have to feel safe
from us,
because, see, if we started to converse,
you might not see me as a terrorist.
You might just see me as a man
who is a son,
a brother,
a friend,
a lover,
and that's dangerous,
because our society
counts on locking up
our sons,
brothers,
friends,
and lovers
to survive

So the next time
you see me,
think it's your patriotic duty
to clutch your purse,
to walk the other way
when walking down the dark alleyway
at midnight,
because I told you...
I'm a terrorist.

Live Better

Brothers and sisters,
don't be in awe of the gems
of the temple,
for they will all crumble.
Get land,
plant seeds,
and build your community.
Brick by brick,
wood plank by wood plank,
build your own
schools,
hospitals,
banks,
army.
Because eventually,
the western society that you stand on,
the western culture in which you put your trust in,
will crumble under your brown feet.
The empirical state of nations rise and fall
with the earth's inhale and exhale.
The tower of Babel will never be completely constructed.
You are putting your faith "in God we Trust,"
but only by His Word will you be saved,
so burn those greenbacks as sacrifice
as you go on your knees in a continual act of repentance.

When you rise from your knees,
build your community gardens
and your African schools.
Lead everyone in building their homes.
Keep your children close to your bosom
because they are your greatest resource.
Live by God alone, because
through Him you are eternal.

Live free to love more,
have more joy,
explore every part of the globe,
because life is what you make it.

The American Empire

The American empire is not your friend.
It is not sweet apple pie,
smiling, big buxom blondes,
and nonstop football and baseball games.
It is not democracy,
freedom,
Christian,
the supreme example of culture to the world.

The American empire does not care for you or about you,
only cares about your one percent overlords.
The ones that stick a foot on the back of your neck
and then slams it deep into a pile of shit.
Until the shit wafts up your nose and overwhelms you.
You taste the shit and then puke the shit,
until you cannot help but swallow the shit
and liking the shit.

The American empire is your pimp.
It has you on your capitalist track
since your first pay check.
It taught you how to produce
from your broken body for its benefit.
You thank it,
when it rips you from your wife and child,
to suck your soul clean
as you wallow in some
office cubicle.

It puts my crippled body on the track, too.
Just gives me less money than you.
Because it cannot manipulate my body
as well as it does yours.
Cannot make me the narrow nose,
pale skinned,
straight-haired man
who can walk and talk normally.
Who it can put in the front reception desk,
when the guests come to visit.

Defectives like me must be dealt with.
The American empire used to lock me up
with a hospital gown
and leather restraints.
No one cared if I shitted myself,
as long as my stench was under lock and key,
away from the main public's noses.

I am not as useful as you.
Your body looks good
for some nice army fatigues.
With some physical training
it can send you to Afghanistan
with a gun in your hand
and a hateful song in your heart.
You can be an integral part
to stomp and break other proud and brown bodies
to the power of its will.

The American empire is not our friend.
It will break us down,
bone by bone,
muscle by muscle,
until nothing is left.

Father Madiba Shook My Hand

He shook my hand,
and as a nine-year-old boy,
my immature mind
couldn't fathom
the rough surfaces
that scraped and scabbed
the hand I touched.

This hand that held
the knowledge of law books
as sledge hammers
that slammed against
the great wall of apartheid.

This hand that embraced and guided
the African National Congress
to express in words
what was on their people's hearts.
Their desire for freedom and self-determination
from unjust white domination.

This hand that was handcuffed
for lashing out against the brutal state.
This hand that was made to break limestone
in an effort to break his spirit
to no avail.
Because this hand was still strong and firm

when he grasped my hand –
after twenty-seven years
of holding cold metal prison bars.

I shook the hand
that crumbled the remnant of apartheid,
and then molded from his country's earth
a democracy that all his people
could thrive and prosper in.

I shook the hand
of the man
honored and admired worldwide.
Now as he rests in peace,
I feel honored and blessed
that he chose to shake mine.

Part Three
Love Notes From A Lonely Krip

When You Left

As I lay here
naked,
about to birth
loved aborted.
I conjure
your scent
as paint
for my mind's mural.

My tongue traces the syllables
of names of our unborn children.
In the plane of dream
of your already absence,
I reconstruct the tome of our affair
to try to untangle my heart
from the nest of thorns
where you left it.

The Problem I Have With You

The problem that I have with you
is you basically used me.
You did not only disrespected me as a man,
you disrespected me as a human.
This was after I offered my home to you
when you were homeless and had nothing.

No one should have the relationship
that we had and deny it.
No one should make love to a person
and then secretly have sex
with someone else the same day.
No one should seriously consider marrying someone?
Then be engaged to someone else,
a few months later.
This is what I know.

But this knowledge is not worth much,
because I did everything to make you stay
and you still left me for him.
But come to think of it,
I am totally fine with you gone.

What Do I Have to Do?

What must I do to get these women to like me?
What do they want for them to be attracted to me?
Do I have to work extra hard
for them to see me as a provider and ideal husband
and not some droopy head, drooling dunce?
What words must I speak so that they will see past
my thin frame of semi-controllable muscles,
slow slurred pronouncement of words,
and powered electric mobility
with augmentative alternative speech?

Do I have to improve myself with my education
and acquire a double Master's or a PhD?
For a slender young thing with a sweet smile
to even take a second glance at me.
Do I have to be fully Professor McLeod
for her to see that I am wise enough
to lead her and our future family?

Do I need to impress these women with money?
Make them moist when I make moves in a Maserati.
If I spoil them with showers of shawls
from Sarah Jessica Parker
will they race to my embrace and mist me with kisses?
Will I impress her as a prince prepared to whisk her away
to her story book ending of her dreams.

Do I need to attract her eye with my body?
Spending hours in the gym toning my muscles
until everything bulges out of me even my manhood,
hard for her pleasure to satisfy
all her carnal lust and desire?

Whatever it is, I have to figure it out quick
because my bed is getting lonely
and I need someone to lay beside me.

Hold On

God, why did you send me her
if you knew you were going to send her away?
Conventional wisdom tells me to let go,
but something in me tells me to hold on.
A small voice keeps telling me it will work out.
Is it you, God?

My Nightmare

So is this where we are?
You jumping from dick to dick
while I keep awake at night
still thinking of you.
As watch the horror flick
Of you laying next to me
But vanish as I reach to embrace you.
Then I see you
as you ride them,
moan for them,
cum because of them.
These images of my night terrors
are my nocturnal company with my insomnia.

How I wish
that I could hold you.
Lay on your bosom
and know
no other head
will rest
where mine has lain.

Place for My Heart
(A Haiku)

Open your palms now!
Let me place my heart in them.
Wrap fingers as its crib.

Father, I Thank You

Father, I thank You for walking with me.
You are always there,
though thick and thin.
You are my constant companion,
my consoler,
my source of joy.
Without You, I am nothing.

Help me walk in the path You set out for me
and not deviate, leaning on my own understanding.
For I know You created me for a purpose
and it is my duty to let Your light shine through me.
Because through my accomplishments,
everyone should see your glory.

Your spirit surrounds me with love
and gives me a peaceful spirit
in the mist of a tempest.
I will always praise and glorify Your Name,
my Lord and Savior, Jesus Christ.

Your Love Is My Harbor

The incessant gnawing in my sleep –
these ideas fly around in my head
biting my brain, tearing my gray, neurological flesh.
I scream in agony in the night
and have only your arms around me as comfort.

Your hands caress and soothe my body,
urging me to sleep
As I lie beside you.
You cradle my heart
and prevent it from ripping out of my chest.

As the endless horror flick of my memories
play through my mind on an endless loop,
you are there to regulate my breath,
Inhale the pain I exhale
as I try to breathe after my torment.

To awake and see your face
is like to see a peaceful shore
after being tossed and turned
in a violent, tumultuous hurricane.
You will always be my harbor after the storm.

Trauma

I will never call you out of name.
But your tongue's razor edge
keeps slicing me with
"cripple,"
"weakling,"
"invalid."
Each time we meet
my cheeks always
laced with ruby scarlet droplets of blood.

You always an image of beauty to me.
Big, black, and beautiful you described yourself.
Always down for that sexy love,
you spoiled me with kisses
that were too sweet for me.
But I ignored the cavities growing inside my molars.

I at first just wanted to help you
when you had no home or no place to run to.
I placed a roof over your head and a bed to sleep in.
I wanted you to depend on me
after I watched the bank stealing your grandma's house,
and I helped you move from place to place.
I knew you had been through it
and needed respite from the storm.

So I gave you comfort in my arms
and you soon found comfort in my bed.

We had unprotected love on the daily,
I had no doubt that you were mine.

But you weren't mine,
you whispered it to me to deaf ears.
Your actions beg to differ though.
Celebrating all day for each of our birthdays,
having a fabulous New Year's Eve dinner together,
a whole-day celebration on Valentine's Day.
You played your part well.

Even with my family not liking you,
I didn't listen.
My mother hated you from jump,
my sisters said you were no good,
and my dad was not impressed.
But still I didn't listen.
Had my blinders on and didn't see you for what you were.
Thought you were my queen,
but you ended up being everyone's doormat.

What did I do to you for you to hurt me like this?
When I thought everything was cool,
you had words demeaning my crippled body
when I tried to embrace you.
It was like something in you
rejected me because of my disability.
Like you thought I was less of a man
because of my disability.

I shared everything with you.
You flew to Minnesota to watch me play power soccer.
You helped me with community and church ministry,
serving at my side.
How could I not think you were with me
through thick and thin?

Should have known something was wrong
when you started fretting about my attendants.
I know one yelled at you and disrespected you,
but he went away.
But you started worrying about my other attendants
even though they did nothing to you.
Always wanting to be with me without them,
even though you knew I needed them.
You stepped up when you were with me
even giving me a shower and feeding me.
I thought I was lucky
and didn't question you on your actions.

When you started critiquing me on the way I run my life
and critiquing my attendants on their work,
I should have checked you,
but I let it slide.
So you got emboldened and lost respect for me.
Finally you dismissed me,
running to the next man's arms,
leaving me in the dust.

To Breathe in Healing

My love, take my hand.
Let's go away from here,
far from here.
Far from the sites
where life struck us
with wounds that wore
our spirits down.
Let's go to our refuge,
where we can pray to our God
and place our burdens in His hands.

We have endured
the verbal, emotional, and spiritual rocks
being thrown even from our family and friends.
We have endured
the frigid night air
as we clutch ourselves
when no one else would.

So when I embrace you now,
I thank God for you
and breathe in the salve
to soothe the lacerations of my heart.

I Just Want Her

God, if You just let me hold her,
keep her safe from harm.
If You let me guide her
into the woman
that I know she is destined to be,
and You let her guide me
into the man
that I am destined to be,
it will be enough.

If You let me walk with her
and share our trials and tribulations together.
Let us dance to each other's triumphs,
it will be enough.

And if You let us lift each other up
while climbing to each other's dreams.
Hold our hands together
as we fly to our goals.
Just being with her
is more than enough.
It is a blessing in itself.

Why You Do Me Like That?

Why you do me like that?
Leave me out in the cold wind,
flapping around like a tattered flag
that you throw away after ample use.

Why you say lies that I don't comprehend?
Like I want to hang around my attendants all day,
as if I prefer them over you, my love.
You can't believe that.

I find happiness being alone with you.
So why you want to stay away from me?
Wave to me in the distance
as I hug myself in the night.

I am not an invalid.
I can hold you close
with my strong arms
and rock you to sleep.

Drowning in Loneliness

When the silence
crowd my throat
in a vice grip
so tight
I can't even whimper.
When goosebumps
rise on my bare arms
and legs
from the incessant wind
whipping against my naked flesh.
It is then I miss you.

When I start to have conversations with my echo
that reverberates against my walls
and comes back to me as an empty shell of my voice.
When my tongue itches to tell you secrets
that your ears are absent to listen to.
It is then I miss you.

When my skin burns for your caress
and stays ablaze in your absence.
When I embrace ghosts in the night air
instead of enfolding my arms on your round frame.
It is then I miss you.

But then I smile
as I remember
that soon
you'll walk
into my arms
again.

My Wedding

My perfect wedding would be in the summer,
when I can go outside and bask in the sun,
dapper in my tux, inhaling the fresh summer breeze.
The ceremony will be at my church at noon,
but it being a West Indian wedding,
it will probably actually start at 1:30 p.m.

All my family will be there:
parents, sisters, uncles, aunts, and cousins
from both coasts of the country, and from Jamaica.
Just to see the union between you,
my beautiful wife,
and I.

You will be in a beautiful white gown
that compliments perfectly my black tux.
When you walk down the aisle,
I will marvel at your sheer beauty,
as you approach me with style and grace.

At the alter we will be locked into each other's gaze,
our tongues inscribing our vows on our hearts.
Our friends and family plainly see
the truthfulness of our love
shining back at them.

When the reverend says, "you may now kiss the bride,"
I smile with heightened elation
before I kiss you boldly on the lips.
At our reception we eat, drink and dance into the night
and then fall into each other's arms on our wedding bed.

Dreams of Her

She will pirouette on the top of clouds.
Her toes will barely touch the airy mist.
She exudes beauty to shine in a crowd.
Our bodies will vibrate with love every kiss.

Her intelligence vibes perfect with mine.
She always knows what to say to please me.
Whether we stay home or go out to dine,
our love will be clear for people to see.

We prayed to enter into each others lives
and God formed us as two halves of one love.
The object of envy of men and wives,
grace will float down on us like a white dove.

So let me keep her safe in my strong arms
and I promise I will keep her from harm.

You Fit

You fit in my clothes like
they were your own.
As if you were meant to be in them.
As if wearing me was your natural attire.

You fit perfectly next to me.
Your curves fit perfectly next to mine.
As if our bodies were two halves of one whole.
As if we delved into each other's souls.

Your words fit perfectly in my ear,
for a perfect resting place for your stories.
As if our minds were vaults for each other's secrets.
As if we serve as sentries for each other's hearts.

Your head fit perfectly on my shoulder.
A sanctuary from a stressful day.
As if we can serve as each other's vacation getaways.
As if wrapped in each other's arms is our own paradise.

The Need of Family

Cup your hands
and don't let your family
slip between your fingers
like sand in an hour glass.
Every family member is precious,
like a ruby sparkling with gold.

No one is meant to be alone,
without kith or kin,
without someone to lean on,
without someone to love you.

See, the lie of rugged individualism
won't nurse you when you are sick,
council you when you are depressed,
or pick you up when you fall in peril.

Yes, no family is perfect,
but a good one will provide
the scaffolding for your life.
A good family will be there
when you need them.

So do not seclude yourself from your family
in some far unreached place
to live a life that you think you want.
Like a fruit separated from the vine,
if you split too long from your source,
you, too, will die.

Perfect for Me

Don't ever trip, thinking that I don't love you.
You will never see me acting brand new.
Like I would go talk to a woman out of the blue
and totally forget you.

Of course not, you are the echo of my heartbeat.
The vibrations ripple out from where our hearts meet.
As we embrace each other naked on these sheets.
I always will hold you and keep you safe.

See, your mere presence makes my soul glide.
I don't care what my mom, my sister, or my father says;
you are perfect for me,
a counterpart whose curves fit perfectly with mine,
whose poetic tongue lyricize with mine.
Let us write our own song,
our own story, together.

Locket

She fuses to me like the other half of a heart locket.
Our love hangs pleasantly around our necks
and lightly on our bosoms.
We encompass our love in our hands,
cup it like a fragile egg that we do not dare let drop.

We kiss our eyelids together,
with our lips brushing lightly on each other's eyelashes.
Our hands spread in the middle of each other's back
while our nipples rub against each other,
as our torsos pass by each other,
as ships in the night
on the sea that is my sheets.

We wrap ourselves in a cloud of secrecy,
away from the outside world.
You lay on my chest.
Your arms dangle around my neck.
Your lips come close to my ears
and tell me secrets you want me to hear.

You are constantly at my back
as we hold each other up,
serve as scaffolding for each other's dreams.
We are the uplift for each other's wings.
We soar high together.

Thirty Minutes

Just wanted thirty minutes of your time.
In between your clients' hair appointments,
hanging out with your clique,
or dealing with your family.
In between your errands
and relaxing in your tub.

Just a brief moment in your busy schedule
to tell you that I love you
and want to spend more time with you.
Want to hold hands in the park
and other cheesy shit like that.
Because with you it won't be cheesy,
but dreamy, to see that you desire me,
as I desire you.

Just hear me out for a second,
and we don't have to talk much.
Let me take your hand and pull you close
as we sway from side to side
to our favorite song,
playing in our heads.

Not the One

I am just not the one.
Even though I thought I was.
Thought I could be your knight in shining armor
your man who could lace you with
all the things you deserve.
Give you that jacket,
        those glasses,
        that dresser
you always wanted.
I will do anything to make you smile.

Your smile flames dimples like florescent lightbulbs.
Your laugh tickles my soul with delight.
To bring you joy has been mine.
An oasis of happiness amongst the sadness.

I want a traditional wedding with all the trimmings.
A bridal party with at least
eight groomsmen
and eight bridesmaids
each.
With both families there,
dressed to the nines.

You want a small wedding.
You, with your purple dress and bare feet,
and your bridesmaids
with purple dresses and bare feet.

Our ideals crash like tidal waves.
No give in the collision
causes one or both to break,
leaving both of us in pieces.

I hold on to you
to prevent the inevitable.
To prevent you from crumbling
in my hands.
I desperately do not want
to join the long line
of those that abandoned you,
but you are not the one.

I wish I could hold your hand
as we go see a Friday premier
of the latest blockbuster movie,
a Madea flick.
But this idea
gnaws and chews
in the back of my mind
that this won't last.
How if we sit in this fetid lap pool
for too long,
we will get sick from the algae
that floats around our torsos.
I don't belong here.

But every time I want to walk out
I see you in me,
me in you.
How everyone abandons us
because of our palsied bodies.
How you and me
created a bubble of solace
together
where all that mattered
was us.
Unashamedly nude,
we found joy
in ourselves
going in and out
of each other's
smooth crevices.

It cripples me
to produce the needle
that bursts this bubble now.

Cuts

My heart bleeds from the cuts
from the sharp machete behind your teeth.
Each word you say
slices at my chest,
burrowing through skin, muscle, rib cage,
until your fork tongue
scrape at my bone.
You say you love me,
and used to talk to me
all throughout my day.
Now I stare at my black, clear phone screen
and it is deathly silent.

My mind plays a torturous movie
I am forced to watch.

You in another man's arms,
your body trembles to his every movement,
like you did with me.
I wake in cold sweats
after night terrors of you calling his name
and I wonder what pain did I cause you
for you to slice my heart up like you do.

Your lying tongue
recite fluffy promises
of how you love me,
how you'll always be there for me.

I try to reach out to you,
but for months now
you are just a mirage in the wind.
Now I am the speck in your mind
that you carelessly flick off
to float helplessly on the ground.

Tired of the Heisman

All I want to do is hold you.
Wrap you in my arms like a blanket,
let your head rest on my chest
so we breathe in unison.
But every time I try to bring you close,
you stretch out both your hands,
knock me squarely in the chest
to keep me at bay.
Like I am trying to tackle you with love
and you have to give me the Heisman
before you slip away.

It is like you hold me for your convenience.
I dry your tears when you come to me
and will love you in sickness and health.
But when you have too much work,
or have an event to attend with your friends,
or have a family emergency,
or just want to be left alone,
your hand jabs firmly against my chest,
only to pull me back
when you feel like it.

Now you say
you want to date other people.
Want to push off on me
like a launching pad
into the next man's arms.

Leaving me to fall head first
and cut my face on the rocky ground,
naked as your aborted fetus.

I try to rise from the rubble to crawl back to you,
but your outstretched palm
is always there to slam me to the ground again.
I promise baby, if you keep on giving me the Heisman,
one day I will just crawl to someone else.

When Death Comes

Hold me in the gaps between your ribs,
tie me like sinew to your bone.
Keep me clenched in your palms,
and squeeze before I drain from you,
like granules of sand between your fingers.
It is you that is the cushion
between the gears that grind me.
See, I spend most of my days
with people who are paid to be with me,
usually locked away in my house.
I watch the sands of time
slide from my window pane,
leaving the remnant of dull brown smudges
that raindrops will not wash off.

You are the sweet speck of gumdrop
on the tip of my tongue
that I suck every drop of flavor out of.
I count the days,
hours,
minutes,
seconds,
when my cheeks
can be cupped by your hands
as you pull me in
to brush your lips against mine.

When my name is ceased to be uttered,
by my mother,
by my father,
my two sisters,
my three attendants,
my many fraternity brothers...,
still keep my name
seared on your tongue,
sweet as a peppermint Life Saver
that you still suck after it dissolves.

When I feel my spirit fading,
and my whole foundation
shaking under my feet,
sweep me off the ground
and hold me to your bosom
until my breath subsides.

What She Does to Me

She wraps me in a cocoon of her love,
insulated from the thorns in my side
that want to leave a bloodstained trail
on the crevice where my hips and thighs meet.
She is the balm that heals the gashes
from stones thrown from life's many assailants.

I find respite in her bosom.
My body,
perceived as broken and useless to others,
is her model of Adonis,
the object of her intimate desire.

My arms become a natural enclosure
where she can rest her weary head
on the glade that is my skin,
like a doe deep in the woods,
secure from a hunter's shot.

We exhale in each other's bodies,
comfortable in each other's naked gaze,
sharing each blemish and scar
we have on our own skin.

We strum each other's hidden organs
and make a symphonic harmony
of our melodic moans.
The cacophony
is a lullaby
that aides us to sleep.

Why You Make Me Smile

Your lips taste like plantains dipped in brown sugar.
I just want to lick the residue off my lips when we kiss.
How I melt in your arms
each time they wrap around my shoulders.
Just sit here on my lap
and let me enwrap my long arms around your torso.
You are not too heavy for my crippled body.
I will not break that easily.

Every time I look in your eyes,
I thank God for sending a woman
that was exactly what I prayed for.
It is He who whispered your existence in a dream
and I just had to wait
until He was ready to reveal you to me.

You walk with sure elegance that even angels admire.
You speak with a wisdom that lingers
in my ear well after you are gone.
Your laugh is such an infectious symphony
that I am happy to play first string in its orchestra.
You know how to calm my spirit
by only saying a few words.

It will be my duty from now on to show you
that I am the man you need and want.
To lead you in the life we want, God willing.
Because I know that by each other's side,
we can do anything.

The Kangaroo Court

I'm already guilty.
You are my judge and jury
and even Johnny Cochran
couldn't get me off.
My crime,
to steal my love
like it was the Crown Jewels.

Not even if I throw myself at the mercy of the court,
it won't change your judgement.
Your verdict is to torture me,
stretch me out on a rack
naked, as you use an oil-drenched whip to lash my back.
Make dripping red gashes
that you never want to heal.

You keep asking your questions.
We already went over
why I broke up with you,
repeatedly, but you want
to imprison me,
and force me
to answer questions
that we both know the answers to.

So lock me up.
Because a full confession
will not satisfy you.

Summer Months

I relished the golden rays
that melt cement.
The gentle caress of breeze
rolls off baked golden hills,
brushing my cheeks
as I cycle my legs on bicycle pedals
or put one braced leg in front of the other.
The laughter of cousins and sisters behind me.

Days free
from the shoulder ache
as arm flings
over guarded keyboards
and eyes squint from the LCD screen gaze.
While I pound out essays on novels,
punch out Algebra and Calculus equations,
and test out biology experiments,
strapped in the chair
of wood and metal.

Long days to stretch limbs
in the back yard swimming pool.
Trap in oxygen between lips
under chlorine surfaces
or to relive stolen toddler moments
to take lone steps in buoyant water.

High school crush came to swim
after six years of school together,
after noticing me in the DC trip Senior Year,
after our graduation,
in a orange patterned one piece.

As we waded,
jacuzzi bubbles encompass torsos.
Arms frail above continuous clear cylinders
that we cannot grasp or hold.
My gaze rests on your pale thighs.

"Go on, you can touch them."

My erratic hand motion
rests on the razor thin leg hairs
of your outer thigh.
First touch of caress,
of mutual sensual sensation,
my palms, so thirsty, had sought quenched.

"If only I didn't have a boyfriend."
The possibilities dashed before my eyes
and I then heard the familiar song of,
"You are so handsome, though.
You will find your own love soon."
I play this song in my head
until it becomes true.

When Flesh Encases Spirit

I cannot divide myself in two.
Flesh fused into spirit
rips my soul in two different directions.
Too double minded to talk,
too scared to utter
those toxic words,
acid to your acid ear drums.

I know you love me;
I care about you too.
But our love scale is not level,
too overburdened with your affection
and too light with mine.

I can't just stay here and watch your heart break.
Each tear you cry
busts a .38 slug in my heart.
I will do anything to make you smile,
even though I know you are not the one.

I keep visualizing us
together naked.
Our dark brown skin
perfectly meld into one.
You on top,
moaning in my ear,
while I rotate my pelvis underneath
in our own cerebral palsy rhythm.

Can't say the words to make it end.
Can't free myself from you
and watch you crumble
as I fly away.

My Lady

My lady —
dark chocolate,
tongue licking,
juice dripping,
full of good loving.

My lady —
hair short and dyed,
colored red and yellow,
fiery like her exuberant personality.

My lady —
dimples with her smile
and a laugh fit for a cherub,
smile stretches across her face,
like her mouth was adorn with the finest ivory

My lady —
your tattoos
canvass your skin
like an epic mural.

My lady —
your name
is always on my tongue,
my mind,
and my heart.

My lady,
my love.

Part Four
The Krip Undress

The Interlude

When we get out
of our wheelchairs,
and you undress me
and I undress you,
I just want to
lick your clit,
make your pussy
soak for my dick,
and I won't stop
until you hop on my cock,
with your titties flapping nonstop
while you moan and groan on top
as we create our own beat
bumping and grinding between the sheets.
Just the way you like it.

Together

Let's just rest here
on these sheets.
Our skin fused into one,
in a body that is ours alone.

Your breasts flatten against my chest.
the rhythm of our lungs sync in unison.
My arms fold around your torso
as your legs straddle my waist.

You release my manhood
from your womb
with a regretful moan.
Not wanting our fusion
to break in any way.

You shiver on my chest,
as I glide my hands
over the length of your back
and caress your firm buttock,
to try to keep you warm.

In the gap between dream
and awareness,
we kiss our dreams
to try to savor each second
of this moment.

You kiss my eyes,
cheeks,
lips,
neck,
chest,
stomach,
until I am washed, cleaned
by your love.

I outline the edges
of your neck and shoulders
with the imprint of my lips.
My arms fold naturally around your waist,
and you squeal with glee
as I give you a squeeze.

Our skin
canvass of desire
we use our lips and tongues
as brushes
to paint the picture of our passion.

We lock eyes
and instantly know
that we belong here.
Our bodies perfectly intertwined,
as two halves
of a love we claim as whole.

Peaceful are we
on these sheets,
until I rise again.
You receive me,
and start this love rhythm anew.

The Eye Undress

I feel your gaze caress my body.
You first notice my eyes,
the intelligent gleam in them.
These brown orbs of intrigue
lock you in.
Our eyes do Morse code with each other,
and let our spirits interpret the messages.

You see how sharp I dress,
the gray fedora on my head tilting to the side,
the H&M sweater on my broad shoulders,
the designer jeans from Express underneath my tray,
the Aldo shoes that shine on my feet –
the feast of me,
both hungers and satiates you.

You look elegant yourself,
in a bright white blouse,
black skirt,
and bright red pumps.

Your eyes revolt your timid chaste nature,
and start to undress me.
You flick off my hat,
tear off my tray,
peel me from my H&M sweater,
unfasten the straps of my chair,
rip off my sweater and shirts.

You can't help but kiss
shoulders and neck.
Your lips quiver as they graze
the tops of my nipples.
Then you slide your body down my legs,
grab one leg to slip off one shoe,
then the other.

You then unfasten my belt,
unzip my pants.
You get me to pivot my hips
and slide my jeans and underwear off them.
You free my rigid ankles from braces,
and squeal with glee as you rip off my socks.

You stand back to view the sight of me.
My arm, leg, and chest muscles twist under your gaze.
You must get your hands all over me.
Massage my feet,
legs,
thighs,
give the long length of my erect penis a few strokes.
Your hands glide quickly up and down my shaft,
and then rub down my stomach and chest.

You kiss my lips,
long and tenderly.
Then turn around,
sit down on my lap,

and help me take off your blouse,
and bra.
You guide my hands
in massaging your stomach and chest.
Your tits perk up to my mere touch,
as you moan a melody in my ear.

You manage to guide my hand,
as we unzip your skirt,
and pull them off with your panties.
My hands cannot help but
slip in and out of you,
until you're moist and wet.

Both naked,
the goose bumps on our skin,
caressed by the wind,
you look back to me,
lock eyes with mine,
and say,
"Make love to me."

But this is only your daydream.

The Test

I am the greatest lover
you will ever meet.
Come test and see.

Don't let my
erratic cerebral palsy limbs,
or my power wheelchair,
or this augmentative voice
that comes out of my iPad,
prevent you
to savor my bulging biceps
coming out of my shirt.
Or prevent you
from the shock of electricity that courses
from your head
all the way down between your legs,
every time I stretch my dimples to smile.

I see you eyeing me across the bar.
I know what runs through your mind.
Are the rumors about men with cerebral palsy true?
Could you handle my erratic motions
gyrating in between your legs?

You want me to roll over to you,
with swagger on point.
Order you a couple drinks,

get you loose off the gray goose,
while I explain,
on my iPad
all the ways
I can satisfy your wettest
desires.

When no one's looking,
you grab my unsteady hand
and slip it down under your skirt.
My finger grazes your lips and clit
as juice drips on the barstool.

Your tongue almost brushs my earlobe
as you whisper,
"Take me home."
I waste no time
to swoop you,
in my van,
to my condo,
where I
bring you to my room,
to finish what I started.

You taste salty and sweet,
at the same time.
But I cannot get enough,
of it on my tongue,
as it lashes and flails

in CP syncopated motion,
against your exposed clit.

Your vagina swallows
my fingers whole,
as they search,
for your buried G-spot.

My hand flutters in and out of you with abandon.
Your lungs almost cannot contain your holler.

You plead for my Jamaican anaconda.
You stoke it rigorously
before I bury it deep inside you.
Our hips slam together like pistons
in a V8.
You voice a symphony of ecstasy
as I make you climax.
Again,
and again,
and again.
When I finish,
you definitely will know,
that I am the greatest lover you will ever meet.

Cameras

Let's play in front of the camera:
you in my t-shirt,
me in my gray pajama bottoms.
We sweat in the glow of the heat lamps.
Click.

You climb onto my bed.
I push you down on the mattress
Help rip my shirt off your torso
to reveal your round breasts and perky nipples.
Click. Click.

I slowly kiss your mouth,
down to your right breast,
down to your stomach.
Kiss each thigh...
Click. Click. Click.
...until I reach your juicy vulva.
Click.

You open your legs wider
to offer me a plate
that I am hungry to devour.
I kiss it
before burying my tongue
in the folds
of clean shaven goodness.
Click. Click.

You moan uncontrollably
as I lick and slurp
copious amounts of your juice
onto my tongue
Click. Click. Click.

When it is my turn,
you lay me out on the bed,
Naked in front of you and the camera.
Click. Click.
You suck my manliness with reckless abandon.
Click. Click. Click.
I close my eyes as I savor every lick of your tongue
on my smooth head.
Click.

When we both have our fill,
I hold you in my arms,
our CP bodies fitting so perfectly
as we hear the sound
documenting our love and passion.
Click. Click. Click. Click. Click.

About The Author

Lateef McLeod is building his career as a scholar and an author. He has earned a BA in English from UC Berkeley and a MFA in Creative Writing from Mills College. He is now a student in the Anthropology and Social Change Doctoral program at California Institute for Integral Studies in San Francisco. He published his first poetry book entitled *A Declaration Of A Body Of Love* in 2010 chronicling his life as a black man with a disability and tackling various topics on family, dating, religion, spirituality, his national heritage and sexuality.

He was in the 2007 annual theater performance of *Sins Invalid* and also their artist-in-residence performance in 2011 entitled *Residence Alien*. He currently is writing a novel tentatively entitled *The Third Eye Is Crying*. More of his writings are available on his website Lateefhmcleod.com and his Huffington Post blog, http://www.huffingtonpost.com/lateef-mcleod/.

Some of his recent community service work includes being the co-chair of the Persons with Disabilities Ministry at Allen Temple Baptist Church and being the chair of the Lead committee and executive board member of the International Society for Augmentative and Alternative Communication. In 2019 he started a podcast entitled, *Black Disabled Men Talk,* with co-hosts Leroy Moore, Keith Jones, and Ottis Smith. The podcast website is www.Blackdisabledmentalk.com,his email address is Lmcleod03@gmail.com